Tatanka • Four Seasons of Custer State Park

Design and Layout by Michael Wolforth

Special thanks to the following people, without whom this book would not have been possible:

Jane, Cody and Michelle Wolforth - The most loving & understanding family a person could ask for.

Dwaine and Najette Tollefsrud - For the idea and photographs, and for a long-lasting friendship.

Steve & Kristi Hilton - For believing in me, and for being there when I needed some help to make this book a reality.

John Hempe - Provided all the captions in the book, and has always been there when I needed help.

Guy Tillett - An excellent wildlife photographer who provided the mountain lion photograph on page 26.

Pete Rosenkranz - A great photographer and friend, for the donkey photograph on page 24.

Craig Pugsley and Custer State Park - For providing the introduction for the book, the branding photo, and the historical photo. Also for the opportunity to photograph the roundup and to be able to enjoy such a beautiful wildlife park.

First Edition May, 2006

ISBN number:0-913062-35-9

Printed by Fenske Media Corporation

For further information about Custer State Park, call (605) 255-4515 or send a letter to Custer State Park, HC 83 Box 70, Custer, SD, 57730

Contents

All captions written by John Hempe

Photographers

Michael Wolforth
Rapid City, SD
605-721-0331

Mike Wolforth is a commercial photographer and Photoshop guru. His love for wildlife began while he was growing up near the Sand Lake Refuge north of Aberdeen, South Dakota. After graduating from high school, Mike traded in his hunting rifle for a camera to capture the wildlife surrounding him. Mike shoots incredible images that he hopes will help educate others about the importance of preserving and caring for our great outdoors and the wildlife that live there.

Photography has also enabled Mike to travel to Ecuador to photograph the poverty, and to Scotland to photograph castles and gardens. Mike now works and teaches in Rapid City. For more than 30 years, Mike's wife, Jane, and their children, Cody and Michelle, have supported and encouraged him in his photography adventures.

Along with being published in numerous magazines, books and publications, Mike's work was featured on the cover of the South Dakota issue of the 2004 24/7 Project. The inside pages of the South Dakota book featured an additional 68 of his images.
I would like to dedicate this book to the memory of Irene Spilde, my late mother-in-law.

Dwaine Tollefsrud
Rapid City, SD
605-716-0847

Dwaine Tollefsrud is a flight simulator technician with Rockwell Collins. He is a lifelong resident of the Black Hills in South Dakota, which he considers to be a very special place. He is an avid outdoorsman who enjoys capturing images of wildlife and nature in South Dakota and throughout the United States. Dwaine is married to a wonderful wife Najette, and they have two children, Jennifer and Erik. He thanks them for their patience, encouragement, and support over the years. Dwaine also thanks Mike Wolforth who made this book happen, John Hempe for the wonderful words that accompany the images, and Steve and Kristi Hilton for their support.
I would like to dedicate this book to my father Selvin and my late mother Doris Tollefsrud.

Introduction

The ground rumbles, the earth shakes, and a cloud of dust appears in the distance as cowboys and cowgirls begin the annual buffalo roundup in Custer State Park, a tradition which began in 1966. Now, some 40-plus years later, this annual roundup attracts far more spectators than the number of buffalo that will be rounded up by park crews. In recent years nearly 9,000 people from around the world have come here to watch modern-day cowboys, cowgirls and park staff saddle up with the hopes of bringing the park's 1,500 head of buffalo safely into the buffalo corrals.

As the cowboys remark, you can herd a buffalo anywhere it wants to go. Some years, the buffalo seem complaisant and the roundup is finished in a couple of exciting hours. Other years the herd is a little more unruly, and it takes several attempts for the wranglers to bring them in.

For the park, the roundup is a much-needed management tool. The animals need to be counted, sorted and vaccinated. The calves are also branded prior to selecting about 350 head to be sold at the live auction the third Saturday in November. All of this is done to keep a balance between the available grassland forage and the number of buffalo the grass will sustain throughout the year, as the park does not supplement the buffalo's food supply.

Custer State Park has played a pivotal role in helping to bring back the bison from near extinction. In 1914, when buffalo numbers nationwide were listed between 500 and 1,000, the park purchased 36 buffalo from the Scotty Philip herd near Fort Pierre. These animals were shipped by rail and ox drawn cart into what is now known as Custer State Park. Through the years, the herd grew and the park obtained more animals from outside sources. In February of 1966 the park offered its first live animals for sale, and from that date on, buyers from around the U.S. and Canada have come to the park to purchase animals to start or supplement their own herds.

Buffalo now number well over half a million in the U.S. and are no longer threatened or endangered. The return of the buffalo is one of several wildlife management success stories that Custer State Park has played a role in. Elk, big horn sheep, pronghorn antelope, mountain goats, and wild turkey are all commonly seen in the park today. That was not always the case, as many of these species were eliminated or nearly eliminated from the Black Hills' borders and beyond. It was through the tireless efforts of South Dakota's Prairie Statesman, Governor Peter Norbeck, that many of these wildlife species were brought into the park and have since helped replenish populations not only here in the Black Hills, but throughout the nation as a whole.

You hear an excited scream as a youngster spots the buffalo in the distance, "Look Mom here they come." Roundup day is a special day in a special place; a place where dreams begin but never end; a place visited by presidents, poets and millions of people like yourself who are here to touch the grass, smell the pines and set their worries free under the star-filled sky of one of America's largest state parks, Custer State Park ... Where the Adventure Never Ends!

Custer State Park Visitors Services Coordinator, Craig Pugsley

Chad Kremer, herd manager of Custer State Park, releases a buffalo into the main arena to be sold during the annual auction held at the buffalo corrals.

Branding also takes place after the buffalo are rounded up.

Historical photo of what corrals looked like in the earlier years of the buffalo roundup.

Buffalo calf waiting to be vaccinated during the winter roundup.

5

TATANKA

Ta-TONK-a
"BULL BUFFALO"

Places to Go - The rear guard of an entire bison herd must have been a familiar and glorious sight to North American Indians whose very survival often depended on the vast herds that once roamed South Dakota's endless plains. Custer State Park's bison herd is one of the largest publicly owned herds in existence today.

WINTER

Winter Powder - Looking like the loser of a snowball fight, this young bison is living proof that Custer State Park is the ideal winter habitat for its massive herd. Winter is no match for the incredible durability of the North American Bison.

Always Watchful - The ice-covered ground does very little to slow the breathtaking speed of the wary antelope. Always vigilant, the antelope herd moves from place to place throughout Custer State Park, ready to flee at the first sign of any danger.

Ice Dancer - Even winter's heaviest frost can't slow the speedy pronghorn antelope, the fastest land animal in North America. Incredibly, pronghorns can reach speeds of up to 60 miles an hour.

The Sentinel (opposite page) - Like a stone wall, a bull stands alone atop an icy ridge somewhere inside the Wildlife Loop. Custer State Park is one of the largest state parks in the United States, attracting over 1.8 million tourists annually from every corner of the world.

Winter Ghosts - Mountain goats are not as visible in the park as the bison, though they are very much there. Silently padding through the winter snow, the park's mountain goats steer clear of the more populated areas in favor of rocky, less-traveled slopes and ledges.

Morning Frost - Scattered across the early morning plains, bison have no problem foraging beneath the frost that blankets the frozen ground.

Snow Capped - Already well-equipped for the harsh South Dakota winters, a curious young calf appears to wear the elements of winter as a badge of courage upon its forehead.

Up in a Meadow Away from the Crowd - When the snows begin to fall and winter is drawing close, the bulls leave the herd to winter alone or in small groups in the back-country areas of Custer State Park.

A Vital Link in the Food Chain - Hunting in deep snow is always a challenge for Custer State Park's coyote population. In a constant search for a next meal, coyotes represent one of the few larger predators in Custer State Park.

It's a Dog's Life - Life is a precarious one for the park's large prairie dog population. Death can come from the sky as well as the ground, as they are highly sought after by the park's many predators, including hawks, eagles, coyotes, bobcats and rattlesnakes.

Tastes Like Chicken - Rabbits abound throughout the park, and are considered a favorite meal for many of the park's predators, such as foxes, coyotes and birds of prey.

Love the Do - Looking more like a rock star than the lord of the plains, this bull is typical of all bulls sporting a thick mane and the shaggy 'hood' that hangs down from the forehead to the muzzle. The hair is primarily for insulation against the icy cold conditions of South Dakota's winter weather, but it also protects the head during inevitable breeding season encounters with other males.

Facing Adversity - Unlike domestic cattle, bison always face into the wind during the harshest blizzards. The bison's thick hide and coat have adapted it to be able to withstand even the most challenging winter conditions within the park.

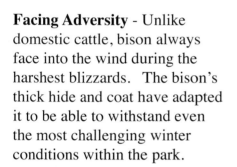

13

Snow Problem - Bison grow thick hair in the winter, and are able to weather winter conditions as low as -50F far better than cattle who sometimes do not survive the worst of the winter storms.

A Harsh Coexistence - South Dakota's winters can reach frigid temperatures as low as -40F, and produce up to 10 feet of snow annually. Both the bison and the crow are ideally suited to a coexistent life on Custer State Park's vast and still untamed plains.

Winter Royal - Within Custer State Park, there are many far away places where the North American Elk prefer to reside. To see one is a not-so-rare opportunity if you're willing to hike to parts less-traveled.

Cold as Ice - South Dakota's winters can be especially hard on its wild inhabitants. As a grazing animal, the bison's diet is made up mostly of grasses and sedges. In the winter, it uses its head and hooves to shovel the snow away from the vegetation.

Winter Roundup - Two prime management objectives within Custer State Park are to maintain a disease-free bison herd and to carefully preserve the integrity of its gene pool. During roundups, the herd is gathered into pens where each bison is tested, given vaccinations, bled for a brucellosis test and tagged for sale. Three times per year the park conducts sales of its surplus animals, which helps to keep the herd's size at a manageable level.

Stare if You Dare - Though not considered a particularly dangerous member of Custer State Park's wild inhabitants, the bighorn sheep can be a formidable attacker when provoked. To stare at one constitutes a direct challenge, which may result in considerably more contact with nature than most people desire.

White on White - Mountain goats blend in very well during South Dakota's winters, both in terms of coloration and in their abilities to 'disappear' into the wild. Their long shaggy coats give them excellent insulation for the harsh realities of the Black Hills' winter conditions.

Madonna and Child in the Wild - (opposite page) Despite their intimidating appearance, bison cows can be very affectionate to their calves. The average calf nurses for one year, and remains close to its mother for approximately three years, after which it fully integrates with the rest of the herd as an adult.

SPRING

Paradise Unpaved - Custer State Park is a veritable paradise for this bluebird, as well as for all of the other wildlife that reside there. With 17,800 acres of rangeland, grazing animals find plenty of space to roam about, and more than enough grassland to go around.

Melody in the Meadow - No wildlife park is complete without the distinctive melody of the meadowlark. The stated mission of Custer State Park is to preserve, protect and enhance the natural, cultural and recreational attributes of the park, considered the 'Crown Jewel of South Dakota.'

Home - Female bison are ready to mate when they are two years old. For the males it takes considerably longer, six to seven years. The mating season begins in July and can run into September.

Not Such a Baby - After a 285-day gestation period, female bison give birth to a single calf that can weigh as much as 40 pounds. A calf is already able to run just three hours after birth, and is weaned from the mother after one year. It will stay with its mother for around three years, after which it will then join the rest of the herd.

19

Nature's Nursery - An adolescent pronghorn antelope fawn keeps a low profile to avoid detection by would-be predators. As the fastest land animal in North America, when the pronghorn reaches adulthood, it will be able to avoid predators by reaching amazing speeds of up to 60 miles an hour across Custer State Park's open plains.

Ladies' Man - Unlike its domestic counterpart, bison do not moo or bellow. Instead they elicit a deep, guttural grunting sound that is very distinctive.

No Worries - A young bison calf wisely stays close to the protective security of its mother. During the fall, when the calves are young, the cows with calves are considerably more dangerous than the bulls.

Here Comes the Rain - Even from the earliest age, the bison is perfectly adapted to its environment on the plains of Custer State Park. Calves are born with a rusty red fur that thickens and grows dark as they mature.

Fast Food on the Plains - Fierce defenders of their young, bison cows are extremely maternal in their basic instincts. The rich nutrients of South Dakota's buffalo grass provide exactly what the mothers need to nurse their calves until they're able to graze on their own.

Born Free - All bison are born with short curved horns, which they will use for defense, and for sparring for status within the herd. At three years of age, this young bison will be a mature adult and will take its place among the rest of the herd.

Something New - Springtime in the park is always celebrated with the birth of hundreds of wondrous bison calves. It is the park's annual goal that 90% of the cows three years and older give birth to calves each spring.

Ears to You - Believed to be the descendents of donkeys owned by early Black Hills settlers, the bands of wild donkeys that roam throughout Custer State Park in search of handouts are definitely a favorite tourist attraction. Despite the fact they are not really very wild, the donkeys will at times bite, kick and knock down an unsuspecting tourist, but usually because they are fighting each other for the roadside buffet provided by passing motorists.

SUMMER

Summer Sun - Summer on the plains can be exceedingly hot and dry. Ideally suited for the harsh realities of South Dakota's winters, the bison seem to be equally adapted for the heat of its summers.

Top Dog ... or Cat - Mountain lions hold a firm position all alone at the top of the food chain throughout the wild lands of the Black Hills region. As North America's largest cat species, this skilled predator has populated the Black Hills at least since Custer's expedition of 1874, during which several sightings and numerous signs were reported.

Creature of the night - It's not a common occurrence to be able to view a bobcat in Custer State Park, though it does happen. Shy creatures that hunt primarily at night, the park's bobcats do help to control the population of small animals and rodents.

The Watering Hole - The North American Bison has made a remarkable comeback since its near extinction in the late 19th century. Today, there are more than 500,000 bison in North America, about 90 percent of which are in privately owned herds. Custer State Park has been auctioning surplus bison to private ranches since 1966, and has had a significant impact on the species' overall recovery.

Stuck in a Rut - For park visitors who come to South Dakota between mid-July and the end of August, they may be able to view the park's bison population during the rutting season. The bulls 'tend' a cow by keeping between her and the rest of the herd. It may last only a few minutes, or as long as several days.

No Respect - Quiet and bashful creatures, mountain goats can be most often viewed around and even on top of nearby Mount Rushmore.

The Shy One - Springtime in the park brings about more than just the birth of its newest inhabitants, such as this young elk calf. It means the rebirth of all of the species there, as the unique blend of populations continues to grow and thrive together as one population that shares one ecosystem.

Size Matters - Massive in its girth, the North American Bison's head is supported by the large hump on its back. The bull's skull plate is extremely thick, adapting it perfectly for the violent impact of fighting other bulls to establish dominance for breeding rights.

Amber Skies - Silhouetted against a deep amber sky at sunset, two young bison patiently await nightfall on the gentle rolling plains of Custer State Park.

Bison Moon - A beautiful daytime moon silently watches over one of Custer State Park's most magnificent residents, as the buffalo cow takes time out to groom itself. The bison's durable coat provides excellent protection from the year-round elements of South Dakota's sometimes extreme temperatures.

Keep a Distance - Bison reach their full weight and size when they are seven to eight years of age. They can be far more aggressive than their grazing demeanor suggests, and sometimes will attack with very little provocation.

The Life of the Party - Bison are considered social animals. Females ordinarily travel in herds of related animals, usually around 60 others, while the males either roam alone or in small groups ... until the breeding season when they join with their selected group of females.

Sunrise Sunset - There are very few places in the world where the western sun is able to cast its searing beauty during an early morning or late afternoon, the way Custer State Park can. The brilliant silhouette of three young bison perched upon a ridge showcases it like no other place on earth.

FALL ROUNDUP

The Buffalo Corrals

Commonly called "buffalo", bison (Bison bison) are North America's largest land mammal, and one of Custer State Park's most valuable resources.

Sometimes called "Lord of the Plains" the buffalo is a unique animal. A mature bull can stand up to six feet high at the shoulder and weigh nearly a ton. Looking very docile as they graze on the open prairie, buffalo can outrun a horse and turn with amazing agility. Stay in or near your vehicle when viewing buffalo. The Custer State Park herd averages about 1,450 animals after the calves are born. The herd is reduced to about 950 animals by public auction.

These corrals are used primarily in the fall when the annual buffalo roundup and auction are held. During the roundup in October the herd is brought into the corrals, calves are branded and females are vaccinated; approximately 500 animals are sorted for sale stock and then tested to meet state livestock regulations.

The bison that will remain in the park are released. Sale stock remain in the corrals until the auction on the third Saturday of November.

Buyers come from all over the United States and Canada to purchase bison from the park for breeding stock or for slaughter.

Together Again - The days of the Old West cowboy are relived every fall at Custer State Park's exciting Buffalo Roundup. A one-day event that attracts nearly 9,000 spectators from around the world, the roundup features the entire park's bison population herded into the Fred Matthews Buffalo Corrals, many of them for auction to ranches throughout the Midwest.

This Land is Their Land - Though considerably smaller in scale, today's bison herd still swarms the rolling hillsides of Custer State Park. It is almost a certainty these days that tourists will be able to locate and enjoy the sight of the herd somewhere within the park.

The Hills are Alive - As the park's herd spills over the rolling hillsides, horseback riders in hot pursuit expertly guide them toward the auction pens where many will be sold to private registered bidders. Before the Plains Indians acquired horses, bison were herded into large chutes made of rocks and willow branches, and stampeded over cliffs.

Togetherness - There's nothing easy about rounding up some 1,500 of America's largest animals, able to turn on a dime as a herd, and run for long distances before tiring significantly.

A Hard Day's Ride - During the roundup, some park officials (pictured is Senior Forester Bill Hill) ride horseback along with other volunteers to help bring the herd of some 1,500 bison into the corrals. When the park's bison are 10 years old, they are taken from the herd. The bulls are hunted and the cows are sold at auction.

Meet the Immovable Object - Custer State Park's older bulls can stand over six feet tall at the shoulders and can weigh over 2,000 pounds. Despite their massive size, mature bulls can run at speeds of up to 40 miles per hour, making them extremely dangerous for tourists who venture too close on foot.

High Tail Means Hightail - Although bison may at first appear docile and unbothered by the presence of humans, park visitors are highly recommend to view them from a safe distance and never approach them. When the tail goes high, there's a good chance it's for you, and you may want to do some hightailing of your own.

Joy Ride Cowboy Style - Few experiences could spike an adrenaline rush quite like sprinting on horseback alongside an earth-pounding herd of bison.

In Flight - Despite being the largest land animal in North America, bison have been clocked at speeds of 40 miles an hour, and can wheel and turn very quickly. It is not uncommon at all for an entire herd to become aggressive in order to defend itself.

Heading for Trouble - The bighorn ram's broad horns and thick skull have adapted it quite well to the very serious contests it must face against other males of its own kind. Though not an everyday occurrence, on any given day in the park, a leisurely drive through may yield the unexpected sight of a cluster of rams browsing side by side.

Lords of the Plains - The Plains Indian became lords of their domain with the introduction of horses by the Spanish Conquistadors in the early 17th century. On horseback, they could literally run down bison and cut them from the herd. As the bison herds dwindled throughout the 19th century, so too did the main food supply of the Plains Indian.

40

Winning the West - Like a scene from
'How the West was Won', modern-day
cowboys ride side by side with the park's
swarming herd. About 25% of the park's
operating budget comes from the annual
sale of bison.

Coming Your Way - Once numbering an
estimated 60 -100 million, bison were the
economical and spiritual focal point of the
Plains Indian. Custer State Park is home
to 1,500 bison and is one of the largest
publicly held herds in the world.

Heard but not Seen - Typically creatures that shun the populated areas of Custer State Park, elk can be seen high atop the ridges throughout the park, especially during the rut season. More often they can be heard though.

Give a Little Whistle - When Custer State Park's elk population goes into the rutting season in the fall, it can be considered a veritable raspy serenade that whistles on for 24 hours a day for several weeks.

Autumn Serenity - Autumn in Custer State Park provides a luscious canvas of greens and yellows, a backdrop painted with forests of cottonwoods, aspens, oaks and locust trees.

On Horseback - For those who participate in the nostalgic ride on horseback, rounding up a massive herd is reminiscent of the cowboys of yesteryear. Custer State Park covers more than 73,000 acres, and is home to some 200 species of animals and birds.

Moving the Herd - Almost like an Old West trail drive, herders ride alongside a group of bison that don't seem to be in a particular hurry to go where the herders want them to go.

Evasive Action - A young whitetail buck frantically searches for cover. At dusk, on any given day, a leisurely drive though Custer State Park's Wildlife Loop will reveal deer casually grazing in fields like domestic cattle.

The Dating Game - While it is true that antelope do have a 'playful' side, the instinct to propagate is a much stronger one. Every autumn in Custer State Park is marked with thousands of high-speed rituals that are integral to the growth and survival of the pronghorn antelope species.

A Sight to See - Thousands of eager spectators throng to the annual fall roundup, hoping for a ringside seat at one of the most spectacular events of the year in South Dakota. The governor of South Dakota himself takes up temporary residence on a designated hill to view the festivities.

All Roads Lead to Bison - One management objective of Custer State Park is to provide public viewing through the numbered road system throughout the park, and by informing the 1.8 million annual visitors of the daily locations of the herd. It would be somewhat rare for visitors to traverse the entire park system and fail to find some portion of the herd.

Tom Terrific - The colorful mating ritual of a Black Hills gobbler is always an entertaining spectacle ... a primitive dance for those fortunate enough to witness it. Since its reintroduction into South Dakota beginning in 1948, the Black Hills turkey population has continued to thrive and grow dramatically into one of the most diverse and healthy populations in the United States.

On Guard - There are few sights quite as magnificent as a regal bighorn ram standing erect on a rocky hillside. Though it's not uncommon to have the opportunity to view one or several of the large rams that patrol the slopes, it is very common to see some of the many ewes and lambs that forage throughout the park.

A Festival of Music, Food and Art - The weekend just prior to the annual Fall Buffalo Roundup always promises to be a uniquely festive atmosphere, highlighted by traditional music, western arts and crafts, and a variety of culinary delights, including the ever-popular chili cook off. Depending on the weather, this event traditionally draws swarming crowds of eager spectators from all around the Black Hills region and beyond, eager to eat, shop and enjoy the sights and sounds of one of most celebrated events in western South Dakota.

Orderly Chaos - Herding bison from horseback produces a thrill few people will ever get to experience. During the annual Fall Buffalo Roundup, more than 50 park staff and volunteers ride herd on the roughly 1,500 bison that populate Custer State Park.

Dry Thunder - Each year, Custer State Park's thundering herd grows to around 1,500 bison just prior to the Fall Buffalo Roundup. Once numbering an estimated 60 -100 million during the end of the pre-Colombian era, the bison population has since dwindled to less than 1,000 in the mid-20th century, and back up to today's numbers of more than 500,000 across the United States.